Energizing Energy Markets: Clean Coal, Shale, Oil, Wind, and Solar

Earning $50,000–$100,000 with a High School Diploma or Less

Earning $50,000–$100,000 with a High School Diploma or Less

Energizing Energy Markets: Clean Coal, Shale, Oil, Wind, and Solar

Connor Syrewicz

Mason Crest

Mason Crest
450 Parkway Drive, Suite D
Broomall, PA 19008
www.masoncrest.com

Printed in the United States of America.

First printing
9 8 7 6 5 4 3 2 1

Series ISBN: 978-1-4222-2886-9
ISBN: 978-1-4222-2894-4
ebook ISBN: 978-1-4222-8930-3

The Library of Congress has cataloged the
hardcopy format(s) as follows:

Library of Congress Cataloging-in-Publication Data

Syrewicz, Connor.
Energizing energy markets : clean coal, shale, oil, wind, and solar / Connor Syrewicz.
pages cm. – (Earning $50,000-$100,000 with a high school diploma or less)
Includes bibliographical references and index.
ISBN 978-1-4222-2894-4 (hardcover) – ISBN 978-1-4222-2886-9 (series) – ISBN 978-1-4222-8930-3 (ebook)
1. Energy industries–Employees–Juvenile literature. 2. Energy industries–Vocational guidance–Juvenile literature. 3. Clean energy industries–Vocational guidance–Juvenile literature. 4. Vocational guidance–Juvenile literature. I. Title.
HD8039.E47S97 2014
333.79023–dc23

2013015558

Produced by Vestal Creative Services.
www.vestalcreative.com

Contents

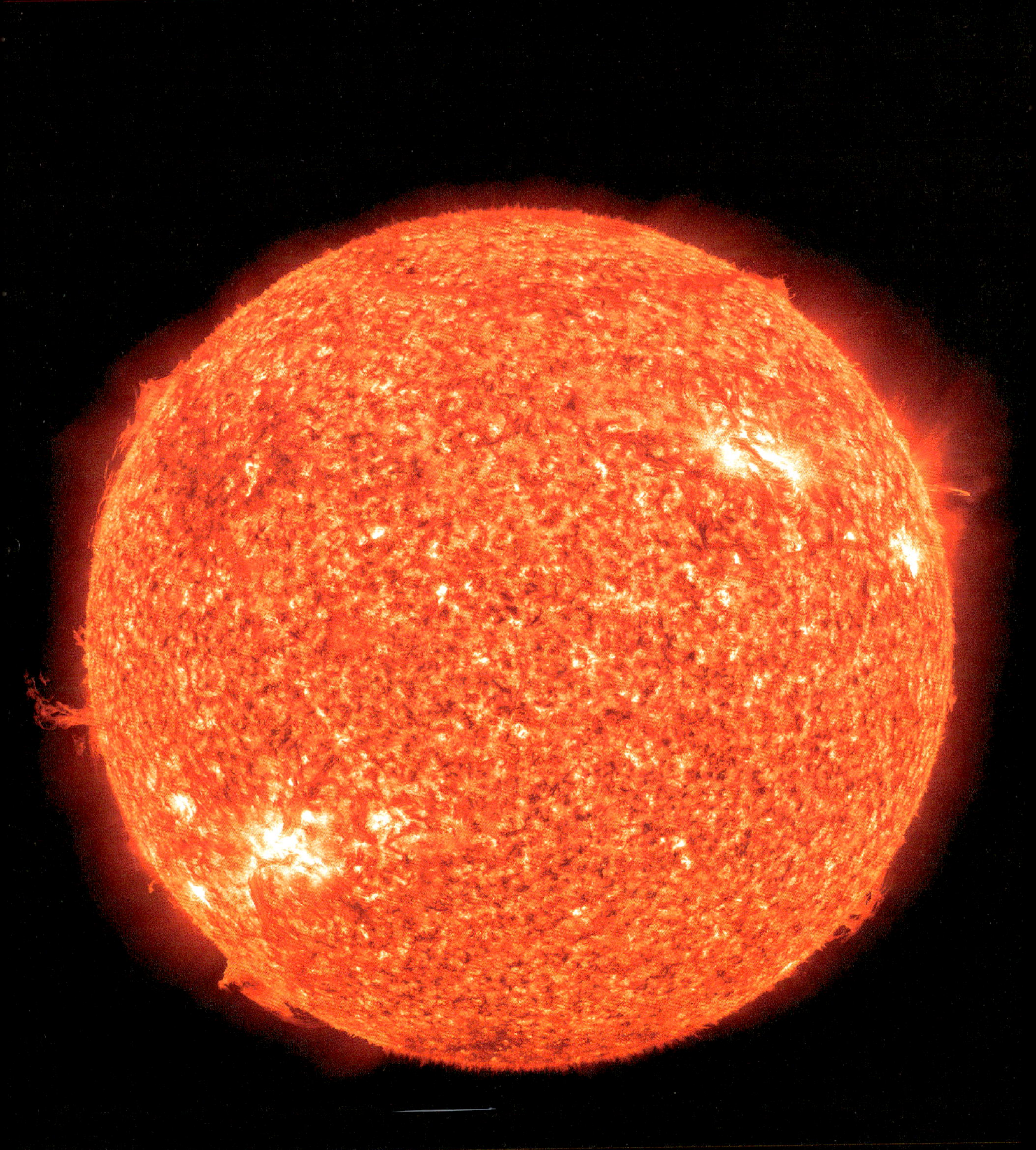

CHAPTER 1

Careers Without College

There is energy all around us. It is vital to our daily lives. Whether it's something as small as a bug flying or as large as the sun revolving around the Earth, every time something moves, it is using energy. Energy is "the ability to make something happen," and we use it every day.

Looking at the Words

The word **biologically** means related to or having to do with living things.

Much of the energy on Earth is stored **biologically**: living things absorb energy from the sun—either directly, through a process called photosynthesis (the way plants turn sun-

Pumps called "nodding donkeys" lift oil out of smaller wells where there is not enough pressure for the oil to flow all the way to the surface. The oil will be used to provide energy for America.

light into food) or indirectly, by eating food—and use this energy to live. While energy in this form has always been available to us, it wasn't until only a few hundred years ago that we learned how to store energy and use it to power just about anything that we need to move. Beginning with the discovery of electricity in the 1700s, energy has become such an important **resource** that we often take it for granted. In the world today, energy powers our hospitals, heats our homes, cooks our food, turns on our lights, and makes our cars run.

Looking at the Words

An available form of help or support is a **resource**. Water, food, oil, people, and knowledge can all be resources.

Something that is **diverse** contains a lot of variety.

The **economy** is the way in which a country or area produces, distributes, and consumes resources.

Making and providing energy for all of these things is the responsibility of men and women employed in what is called the "energy sector." The energy sector represents a large and **diverse** number of careers: electricians, scientists, lab technicians, heating and air-conditioning mechanics, engineers, technicians, and oil and gas workers like roustabouts and derrick operators, to name only a few. These men and women have careers that are necessary for the entire **economy**; almost no other industry would be able to operate without the energy sector!

While some jobs in the energy sector are highly technical and require a college education, a large number of these well-paying careers require little more than a high school diploma, determination, and a passion for the exciting work that it takes to keep the world energized!

The College Question

"Not going to college," says Nicholas Wilsey, "was a tough decision." Nick is a rotary drill operator whose family has been working in the oil and gas industry for almost sixty years. Nick has only been working the industry for the past five years, but he was recently promoted from a roustabout—a general field worker who inspects and repairs equipment, among other duties—to a rotary helper—a position responsible for the day-to-day oversight of a natural gas or oil drill.

"My family didn't push me into the oil industry," Nick says. "We make okay money so I could have gone to college if I'd wanted to. I wouldn't have had to take out loans."

Although Nick didn't have to worry about money when he was making his decision, finance shapes many young people's decisions when considering whether or not to go to college. CNN reported that the average student in 2012 graduated college nearly $27,000 dollars in debt, a debt that takes about ten years on average to pay.

Nick's older sister, Jenna, went to college for business, and her experience of trying to find a job after graduation was a big factor in his decision. "Jenna ended up back to work at the oil field," he says. "We started at almost the same time, even though I'm almost six years younger. She had a good time at college, but it didn't really get her anywhere in terms of work."

As Jenna discovered, in certain fields, many young adults have a hard time finding employment. The Bureau of Labor Statistics reports that professional and business services have been one section of the economy that, since 2008, has been experiencing high unemployment. Periods of high unemployment in an industry mean that there will be more experienced **candidates** searching for a smaller number of job openings, and people new to the industry may have a difficult time acquiring **entry-level** jobs.

"I went to college without really knowing what I wanted to do," Jenna says. "I just assumed I'd be able to use business skills wherever I work, and I thought having a degree would be the best way to make sure I could get a job. But, after I graduated, I spent a year looking for jobs. I finally gave up. Going to work at the oil fields with my brother wasn't so bad. We practically grew up there."

Jenna's experience after graduating isn't very different from that of other recent college graduates. According to CNN, half of all college graduates are either unable find a job or ended up finding a job for which they didn't even need a college degree.

Jenna's business degree did help her eventually, though. Because of her degree, she was promoted to a management position in the oil company. Despite her new position, however, her salary isn't very different than Nick's. "As a rotary helper," Nick says, "I make $37,000 a year. In the offices, Jenna makes about $40,000 a year. But I plan to catch up to her!"

Looking at the Words

People who are **candidates** are being considered for a job.

An **entry-level** job is one that requires minimal experience, and is the first step in a career.

Learning Outside the Classroom

Another important factor in Nick's decision to skip college was his father's experience. Nick grew up watching his father work as an oil and gas worker. "My dad started out exactly where I did. By the time I was

These men are taking community college classes that will qualify them for entry-level positions in various energy jobs.

born, he was making good money as a rotary drill operator." Rotary drill operators oversee teams that operate, inspect, and repair drills and gas wells on a daily basis.

"When I was in high school," Nick says, "a lot of my friends were going to college. I wanted to go but for all of the wrong reasons. I wanted the college lifestyle but didn't care about the work or getting educated. I finally decided that wasn't a good enough reason." Nick wasn't sure what he would have studied in college if he had gone. "I was interested in theology and philosophy—but I didn't have a clue what I could do with majors in those subjects. Mostly, I just liked reading theology and philosophy books—and I could do that at the library, without going to college."

Like most young adults, Nick talked to his parents about his choices. "I told my parents that I really didn't know what I wanted," Nick says. "They would have been fine if I decided to go to college—but my dad also decided to take me down to the field where he works. He talked about all the different jobs I could get working there. I thought about it a lot. I decided that it just made more sense to start making money doing something right in front of me, instead of heading off to college. Especially since I didn't have a clue what I wanted from a college education."

Not everyone is lucky enough to have a family member or friend who can help young adults explore a particular industry, but all young people facing a decision should do what Nick did: Explore the options. Read all you can about various careers, both in the library and online. Talk to the adults in your life. Ask questions. You may find out you have options you never realized.

"One of the best things I ever did," Nick says, "was take time to learn about the industry. Up until then I kind of took it for granted. It was just what my dad did. It wasn't something I'd ever thought about doing myself. But when I finally made the decision not to go to college, I felt good about it. I didn't feel like there was anything I'd be missing"

Some oil fields are located offshore, in the ocean, where rigs like this are used to pull oil from the Earth and transfer it to ships.

Nick understood his options. He didn't make any decision without taking the time to carefully consider and understand each one. And he didn't only explore the gas and oil industry; he also talked to electricians and truck drivers about their careers. "I knew I wanted to do something that was hands-on," Nick says. "I love reading, but I also like doing physical stuff. I followed an electrician around for a few days while he did service calls and repairs. I talked with some truck drivers about their lifestyle. I went to a construction yard and talked to some workers during their break. Everyone was really nice. They were all happy to talk to me. They told me what they liked about their jobs, and what they didn't."

During this time, Nick also talked to his sister about the benefits of a college education. He didn't want to feel like he had missed out on something important. He knew that college is often the first experience that many young people have of living without the safety and security of their parents. Going to college also teaches many "soft skills," like communication, compromise, and **flexibility**. Learning these things can be very important for a young person.

After taking the time to consider many different careers, both those that required a college education and those that did not, Nick was able to make his decision with the confidence that his choice would be the best one for him. According to Nick, oil and gas work had everything that he was looking for: a good paycheck, job security, hands-on physical labor, and the feeling that he was contributing to his community. "In my humble opinion," Nick says, "energy is the most important field there is. Think about it. Every time I see the streetlights turn on, I get this little

Looking at the Words

Flexibility is the quality of being adaptable and willing to change.

A job installing solar panels is an interesting career that improves homeowners' quality of life while also protecting the environment.

thrill. Maybe it sounds stupid, but I really feel like the work I do makes a difference in the lives of everyone I know. I feel pretty good about it."

Nick's key to success was exploring all his options with an open mind. He spent a lot of his free time learning about different careers, and he dedicated himself to getting educated about education.

Should you go to college? It is an important question. No matter what career path you decide to take on in your life, you're going to have to be willing to learn and work hard. So it makes sense to pick a career that's the right one for you, one that you'll find truly fulfilling. Ask yourself: "What do I love to do? What are my hobbies? What do I have a passion for? What are my options? Do I need to go to college to get the skills that I need to be successful? How can I eventually earn a living doing what I love?" Only you know the answers to those questions.

175 TONNE

CHAPTER 2

What Do Workers in the Energy Sector Do?

In the past, burning fossil fuels was one of the only ways for the energy sector to make energy. Fossil fuels are the remains of biological life, mostly plants and bacteria, which have been decomposing in the

Looking at the Words

Sources of energy that are formed from the remains of living things are called **fossil fuels**. Some fossil fuels include oil, coal, and natural gas.

ground for millions of years. People employed in the coal, shale, and oil industries extract these **decomposed** remains and turn them into the fuels we use every day. These industries are known as the "non-renewable" energy sector, because the amount of fossil fuel available to us is limited. This means that, eventually, we will run out of fossil fuels to make energy.

Burning fossil fuels is the easiest, cheapest, and (in much of the world) most widespread method of producing the energy we need—but burning fossil fuels also has a number of harmful side effects. The most damaging of these side effects is that burning fossil fuels pollutes Earth's atmosphere by filling it with chemicals known as greenhouse gases. Greenhouse gases, on their own, are not harmful to our atmosphere. In fact, they are responsible for holding on to a lot of the heat the Earth receives from the sun. But when too much of these gases are present in our atmosphere, too much of the sun's heat is held in. This process goes by the name "global warming," and it is one of the major environmental issues facing the world today.

Looking at the Words

Something that is **decomposed** has died and decayed.

Governments, scientists, industries, and individuals around the world have slowly begun to tackle the issue of global warming. One way is through the development of "alternative" energy sources like solar and wind power. The men and women responsible for making and providing energy from these alternative energy sources are employed by a much smaller part of the energy sector known as the "renewable energy sector." Wind and solar energy are renewable energy resources because they allow us to make and store energy; unlike fossil fuels, energy from renewable resources can never be used up—and they do not add to the amount of greenhouse gases in the atmosphere.

Coal, gas, and oil are all fossil fuels. One day, we may no longer depend on these nonrenewable energy sources—but for now, they are still important parts of the energy industry. Each one offers many types of jobs.

Coal

"Whether we're talking about a fossil fuel or an alternative energy," says Susannah Chanin, an electrician with over twenty years of experience, "at some point, it is going to be electricity."

Electricians, who repair and maintain electrical systems, are on one of the many important career paths within the energy sector. Electricity is the form in which energy is delivered whenever we plug something into a wall outlet or put a battery into a piece of mobile electronics. As a result, electricians can work anywhere from homes and apartments to industrial buildings. They have a hand in the design of just about anything that runs on electricity.

Susannah spent the first half of her career working as a **residential** electrician while working part time as an electrical technician for a coal power plant. Susannah has spent the last ten years converting electrical systems to alternative energy sources like wind and solar technology.

"Most people," Susannah says, "don't realize that coal is the main way the United States makes electricity. We burn over 2.5 million tons of coal each and every day."

Looking at the Words

An area that is **residential** is designed for people to live in.

One of the enormous machines that extracts coal from the Earth.

Looking at the Words

The act of taking something out using force is called **extraction**.

The coal industry refers to the **extraction** of the fossil fuel coal from the ground so that it can be burned to generate electricity. The coal industry operates by a three-step process: mining, shipping and, processing. For every step, there are many well-paying jobs that someone without a college education can attain. According to ONET OnLine, some of these jobs include:

- **Mine cutting and channeling machine operators** operate machinery such as plows, and cutting machines to cut or channel

along the face or seams of coal mines, stone quarries, or other mining surfaces for blasting, separating, or removing minerals or materials from mines or from the Earth's surface.

- **Continuous mining machine operators** operate self-propelled mining machines that rip coal, metal and nonmetal ores, rock, stone, or sand from the mine face and load it onto conveyors or into shuttle cars in a continuous operation.
- **Tank car, truck, and ship loaders** load and unload chemicals and bulk solids, such as coal, sand, and grain into or from tank cars, trucks, or ships using material moving equipment.
- **Heavy and tractor-trailer truck drivers** drive a tractor-trailer combination or a truck and transport goods or resources from one location to another.
- **Crushing, grinding, and polishing machine setters**, operators, and tenders set up, operate, or tend machines to crush, grind, or polish materials such as coal.
- **Power plant operators** control, operate, or maintain machinery to generate electric power.

The "processing" stage of coal production is very important. This stage refers to treating and burning the coal that has been extracted from the ground.

"Clean coal" refers to a particular way that coal is burned in a power plant. Most power plants in America today have technologies that limit the amount of greenhouse gases produced-by burning coal. This means that while burning coal is still

Looking at the Words

Greenhouse gases are substances that trap heat in the earth's atmosphere. Greenhouse gases are causing climate change.

polluting our atmosphere, we harm the environment significantly less by using this method.

Gas and Oil

While coal is the main resource used in the production of electricity, gas and oil are other forms of fossil fuels that are extracted from the ground in order to generate energy.

Natural gas is a fossil fuel that is sometimes extracted from shale rock formations using a **controversial** technique known as induced hydraulic fracturing—a process that pushes chemicals into dense rock in order to push out tightly held natural gas. Many people worry that the process of hydraulic fracturing is dangerous to the environment and to human health; however, these findings are often doubted or contested. Like coal, natural gas is very widely used for generating electricity, but it is also used in the manufacturing of many other products, such as plastic.

Looking at the Words

A situation or person that is **controversial** causes a lot of disagreement.

Oil, on the other hand, is a fossil fuel used mostly to generate power for our vehicles. The process by which it is extracted from the ground involves digging a well, installing mechanized pumps, and then refining this raw or "crude" oil into a form of fuel—gasoline, diesel fuel, or jet fuel, for example. Even though America uses about 23 percent of the oil produced in the world, it only produces about 10 percent. This means that some of the oil we use needs to be bought and imported from other countries.

The process by which these fossil fuels are burned to create energy is generally the same as it is for coal: extraction, transportation, processing, and burning. As a result, careers like truck drivers and power plant operators are available in all fossil fuel industries. The Bureau of Labor Statistics and ONET OnLine list some other jobs, specific to the gas and oil industries that do not require a college education to attain:

- **Roustabouts** clean equipment, keep the work area orderly, inspect pipelines to locate leaks, move and install pipelines
- **Derrick operators** Inspect derricks, or order their inspection, before they are raised or lowered. Derricks are large cranes used in the construction of gas or oil well.
- **Service unit operators** maintain wells by removing tubes or rods from the hole that is drilled into the ground,
- **Rotary drill operators**, also known as drillers, oversee maintenance of the drill rig and implementation of the well plan and train crews and introduce procedures to make operations safe and effective.
- **Petroleum technicians** provide support to scientists and engineers in exploring and extracting natural resources, such as minerals, oil, and natural gas.

Solar and Wind

Renewable or "alternative" energies make up a very small portion of the energy market. In 2011, only 14 percent of all energy generated in the United States was from a renewable resource.

"I've always cared about the environment," Susannah says, "but I never knew how to get involved. I felt helpless. So I love my job now." Once the U.S. government started funding alternative energy projects

A row of solar panels at a solar energy plant.

like wind and solar energy, Susannah found a way to put her skills as an electrician to use.

Unfortunately, because only certain states are significantly expanding their funding for alternative energies, Susannah had to move in order to work on these projects. The states of Iowa and North Dakota generate more than 10 percent of their electricity supply from renewable resources. California, where Susannah moved, is also developing both wind and solar energies.

"Alternative energies are exciting," Susannah says. "Every day, I help make the world cleaner and healthier." She also enjoys the hands-on experience of working with alternative energies. "Oil is going to run out eventually," she says, "and I, for one, want us to be prepared." Her main role now is overseeing projects to update "power grids"—systems of wires that deliver power to a particular area—so that they will be compatible with the new and extra energy generated by renewable resources.

Wind power refers to the process by which energy from wind is converted to other forms of useful energies. This conversion process begins when wind pushes the blades of wind turbines—windmills built to generate large amounts of energy. Wind power, as an alternative to fossil fuels, is plentiful, renewable, widely distributed, clean, produces no greenhouse gas emissions during operation, and uses little land. Wind power wasn't considered dependable due to the inconsistency of weather patterns, but today modern forms of wind power generation take these issues into consideration and have created solutions for them. The only problem that remains is the fact that many people do not like the look of large turbines. Community-led efforts have tried to stop the construction of wind turbines near residential homes, despite the price and environmental benefits of wind power.

Solar power, on the other hand, refers to a method of capturing and conversion of the sun's rays directly into electricity. This energy is captured by a technology known as "photovoltaics"—metals that have

specific properties that make the conversion process easy. Like wind energy, solar energy was at first considered to be not very practical because of the inconsistency of weather patterns, but recent developments in technology have helped solve this issue. The six largest solar power plants on Earth are currently being built in America, five of which are located in California.

Many careers for high school graduates are available in these fields. According to the Bureau of Labor Statistics, these careers include:

- **Engineering technicians** assist engineers with solving technical problems in research, development, manufacturing, construction, inspection, and maintenance.
- **Semiconductor processors** turn semiconductors into photovoltaic cells.
- **Coating and painting machine setters, operators, and tenders** apply coatings to solar panels, which can be a complicated process that must be done with a high level of precision.
- **Welding, soldering, and brazing workers** apply heat to metal pieces during the manufacturing process, melting and fusing them to form a permanent bond.
- **Wind techs** are responsible for both regular maintenance and performing complicated repairs of wind turbines. The average workday is spent climbing and inspecting multiple turbines
- **Wind turbine service technicians** do much of their daily maintenance work in the nacelle, where the gears and sensitive electronics are housed.

Renewable versus Nonrenewable Energy

The most obvious disadvantage of working in the oil, gas, and coal industries is the part that these industries play in polluting our atmosphere. But these three industries combined produce 86 percent of all the energy generated in this country. They are much larger industries than wind and solar, and, as a result, they have more jobs to offer.

Looking at the Words

Having a high chance of keeping your job is called **job security.**

Wind and solar energy, on the other hand, are expanding industries, which means that new positions will open quickly. If funding from the government does not decrease, workers in renewable energies will also enjoy good **job security** and the benefit of learning valuable skills in advanced technologies.

There are no significant financial benefits of working on one side or the other; there are men and women making over $50,000 a year working in almost every career mentioned in this chapter!

CHAPTER 3

How Can I Work in the Energy Sector?

"One of the best things about this sort of work," says Emmanuel Phillips, a power plant operator, "is the sheer number of jobs out there. Almost all of them are hard work, though. Not everyone is cut out for it. But if you like working with your hands, there are lots of opportunities. You could also operate heavy machinery—which can be a lot of fun. And we need computer people too." Emmanuel works at a power plant that processes

Accurate depth-perception is important for operating this machinery that digs coal from a mine.

energy from both wind and coal. His plant is located in Texas, the state that generates, by far, the most amount of wind energy of any state in the U.S.

According to Emmanuel, most people who work in the energy sector are detail oriented and work well in teams. "We need to pay attention to details," he says, "because one small mistake could either ruin a piece of expensive equipment—or hurt someone really bad. Believe it or not, team players do better. You watch each other's back. If something slips by one guy, the next one catches it. So you gotta enjoy working with others. This isn't a job for loners."

Is Working in the Energy Sector Right for Me?

"Not everyone may be right for this kind of work," Emmanuel continues. "It's hard and it's dangerous. You're working around heavy machinery and high-voltage electricity. A small mistake can kill you. Wind-power workers have it the worst. They have to climb a hundred feet or so whenever a wind turbine needs maintenance. My brother tried to do the job, but he couldn't handle the heights."

Emmanuel's advice: Young people who are interested in the energy sector need to ask themselves, "Are these jobs right for me?" Whether you are drilling for natural gas or maintain wind turbines, most entry-level jobs in the energy sector, require a certain amount of physical labor. The Bureau of Labor Statistics lists some other skills that are important to these kinds of careers:

- **Depth perception**: you need to be able to judge distances accurately when you're moving heavy machinery. The safety of other workers may depend on it as well.

A natural gas drill; natural gas is a growing industry.

- **Detail oriented**: energy-sector workers use equipment that must be carefully watched. Engineers need the information collected by monitoring gauges to judge the effectiveness of operations.
- **Eye-hand coordination**: these workers need an ability to move large pieces of machinery or equipment into exact placement, so their eyes and hands need to work well together.
- **Interpersonal skills**: these workers operate in teams, so listening to and interacting with other team members and supervisors is important.
- **Physical strength**: energy-sector workers must have the strength to move heavy equipment, materials, and machinery.

While these are skills needed by anyone who will be doing physical and manual labor, many other skills are needed by anyone who will be in a management position, such as a power plant operator. According to the Bureau of Labor Statistics, power plant operators need many skills, including:

- **Diligence**: power plant operators, distributors, and dispatchers must be careful, attentive, and persistent.
- **Mechanical skills**: power plant operators, distributors, and dispatchers must know how to work with machines and use tools. They must be familiar with how to operate, repair, and maintain equipment.
- **Problem-solving skills**: power plant operators, distributors, and dispatchers must find and quickly solve problems that arise with equipment or controls.

Certain other skills will be needed, depending on the particular energy career you pursue.

If you already have some of these skills, you are already well on your way to one of the many exciting career in the energy sector. If you are not very strong in some of these areas, now is the time to begin to learn and explore ways to develop your abilities.

Pennsylvania is funding community college programs like this one that teaches entry-level roustabout skills. The state predicts that there will be over 32,000 job openings in Pennsylvania's energy industry by 2016.

Becoming an Energy-Sector Worker

While the energy sector offers many exciting opportunities to someone without a college education, if a person in this field wants to be successful, she has plenty she will need to learn. Many of these skills are learned on the job. Others might be learned from an apprenticeship or vocational school.

"You need to have at least graduated from high school to get pretty much any energy job," Emmanuel says. "I use stuff I learned in school every day. Math. Science courses like geology and earth science. I work with a guy who went to a special high school where they focused on machine work. I grew up in New York State, where they have BOCES classes that teach practical stuff. Taking classes there really helped me out."

A vocational school, also known as a technical school, can also be a great alternative to college for people interested in working in the energy sector. Vocational schools offer training in a specific set of skills for a specific industry. They are much cheaper than a college education and usually much shorter—generally between six months and two years, depending on what kind of career you would like to pursue. "I went to a technical school after high school," says Emmanuel. "It lasted less than a year and cost only a few thousand dollars. Counselors from the school worked with employers to find me the job I have now. I finished free of debt. And I was employed within a couple of months. Most of my buddies who went to college can't say as much!"

Another way to work in the energy sector is to apply for an apprenticeship. While apprenticeships are only available in some careers, for other careers, like electricians, beginning as an apprentice is the only

Land near volcanos has good access to geothermal energy. This borehole house in Iceland pulls the heat from within the Earth to be turned into electricity.

Geothermal Energy

Another renewable source of energy is known as "geothermal energy." The center of the Earth is made of an extremely hot mixture of melted rock and gas. The closer you are to the core of the Earth, the hotter it gets. Burning below us, every second, is a source of energy that could last forever!

Geothermal energy captures steam—evaporated water—from very hot underground collections of water or reservoirs. While the technology to capture this heat is available commercially, its use is still limited due to existing infrastructure—wires and pipes hidden underground—and the rarity of these hot, underground reservoirs.

way to get hired. Apprentices usually have very little prior experience. They are hired by a company in order to be taught while they work. Apprenticeships are usually longer than a vocational school, about four years, and sometimes involve classes at local community colleges.

No matter how you get the skills that you need, compared to a college education, the investment of time and money is pretty small!

This oil refinery in Washington State produces 115,000 barrels of oil per day and employs 350 people.

A job on an oil tanker will mean you will work away from home for long periods at a time.

and need to work their way up to higher-paying positions, like the one that Mark has now. This is true for virtually every industry in the energy sector—and while this means that making great money requires a lot of hard work, it also means that making great money is possible no matter what kind of education you have.

High-Level Earnings

Mark has been a rotary drill operator for over fifteen years. He says, "I have a great job. I work with heavy machinery, which is pretty exciting. I like the challenge. And I make great money doing it."

A drill rig requires someone with accurate driving skills.

Mark climbed as far as he could go in the gas industry. Now, however, he admits he is getting somewhat old for his current position. "My managers are talking about bringing me into the office. I'd work there for the last few years before I retire. I hate to think I have to give up what I do—but I also don't want to cause an accident. You see it in some of the older guys. When they start to get older, their depth perception starts to go. You don't want to be driving a big machine and run it into a building because you misjudged the distance."

Mark has been offered the same salary he makes as a rotary drill operator, $64,000 a year, to work as an office manager.

Electricians have a very similar pay system to that of oil and gas workers. An electrician starts as an apprentice making 30 to 50 percent

This is a large and powerful portable rig used mostly for deep drilling into solid bedrock.

Power plants convert various kinds of energy into electricy. This plant uses the energy from running water.

A coal-powered power plant in Virginia.

the salary of a fully trained electrician. Pay raises are given as she learns. The top 10 percent of electricians make over $80,000 a year!

Other high-paying careers in the energy sector include power plant operators, the top ten of which earned over $88,000 a year; machinists, whose highest-paid workers make over $60,000 a year; and mechanical engineering technicians, whose top earners bring in over $73,000 a year.

This is only a sampling of some of the fantastic salaries that high school graduates make given the right mix of determination and problem-solving skills!

A typical nuclear power plant employs 400 to 700 workers.

Average Salaries

Making over $64,000 dollars a year is certainly not impossible for any energy sector worker who is willing to become experienced and work hard, but Mark makes an exceptionally high salary for a rotary drill operator. This is, in part, because of how long Mark has spent in the position, but it is also because of where he works: on a drilling rig in the middle of the Gulf of Mexico. "Whenever I go home, it's a boat ride that takes a few hours," he explains. "So I spend a lot of time away from family. It's really more of a lifestyle than a career. But the money's great."

The average rotary drill operator makes, on average, $51,000 a year. But the average for all oil and gas workers—including roustabouts, service unit operators, and derrick operators—is $37,000 dollars a year.

Many of the average salaries in the energy sector are much higher than this. Petroleum technicians, for example make $54,000 a year on average, and the salary of power plant operators is even better: $65,000. These, however, are very difficult positions to get. Someone hoping to get these positions will need to start at a position and salary much lower than this.

Most of the average salaries in the energy sector, such as those for wind turbine technicians, machinists, and mechanical engineering technicians, are comparable to those of oil and gas workers. But when you consider that even the average salary for all oil and gas workers is a few thousand dollars above the national average for all jobs, including those that require a college degree, the careers available in energy are still fantastic, well-paying options to consider.

CHAPTER 5

Looking to the Future

The job outlook for most careers in the energy sector is bright. Energy is needed by every other industry in the United States; therefore, at no time in the near future will the need decline. On the contrary, the need for energy is growing rapidly!

Of all these careers, the outlook for electricians is perhaps the brightest. According to the Bureau of Labor Statistics, the number of electrician jobs between 2010 and 2020 will grow 23 percent, much faster than the average for all jobs.

The rapid need for electricians is, in part, because of the growth of alternative energies. As fossil fuels are used up, new energy sources will need to be created—and this means

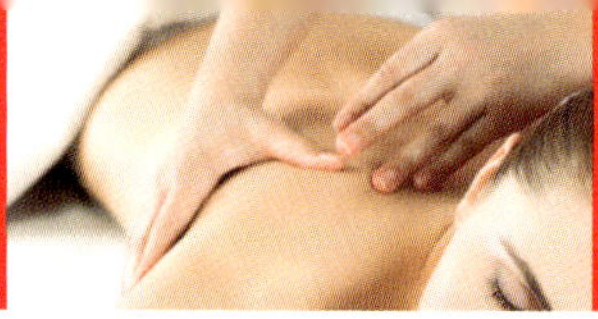

Maintaing power lines creates many jobs.

Wise Words

"To accomplish great things we must not only act, but also dream; not only plan, but also believe."
Anatole France

"Commit yourself to your own success and follow the steps required to achieve it."
Steve Maraboli

"Our work is to discover our work and then with all our heart to give ourselves to it."
—Buddha

that new electrician jobs will open quickly in order to handle all of the work that it takes to link these new power sources to homes and power grids.

The growth of alternative forms of energy is helping keep many industries alive. Job growth of mechanical engineering technicians, for example, is only 4 percent in most industries, very slow compared to all other jobs. But many new jobs for technicians are being generated by the development of alternative energies and the need to manufacture parts for these industries.

Do You Have a Passion?

There's a lot of talk about passion these days: "Find your passion… Pursue your passion… Do what you love…" But passion, it turns out, lives in all sorts of places. There is only one real formula: try things. Try things and see how they fit. Try jobs and find out what you like—and just as important, find out what you don't like. Passion can come later. Right now, just find something you enjoy. That's a starting point. Maybe it'll become that thing you can do for hours and it feels like only a few minutes have gone by. But don't put that pressure on yourself. Start small.

Adapted from the essay "The Truth About Finding Your Passion" by Colin Ryan. More of his work can be found at his website: http://astanduplife.com.

Advancement and Skills

Advancing in the energy sector is consistently a matter of hard work, but the opportunities vary from career to career. For example, oil and gas workers are expected to move through the ranks with promotions, and a determined person can quickly find herself advancing through all of the possible jobs in the oil and gas industries.

There are more than 1700 natural gas plants like this in the United States. According the Natural Gas Caucus, 622,411 jobs are directly created by the natural gas industry, along with 723,102 indirect jobs such as support people and clerical workers.

Natural gas companies also need managers and clerical workers to work in office complexes like this.

Wind turbine technicians or machinists, on the other hand, will have a difficult time advancing because of the relatively small size of the alternative energies industry. Some advancement opportunities will become available as the industry grows; however, most of these opportunities will involve moving from manual labor to management. Any worker interested in managing should prepare himself with business and business management courses in order to show he has what it takes to lead a team.

Even though advancement isn't possible for every career, at least no energy sector worker will have to worry too hard about losing their job. Knowing you have a secure position at a company and that you won't be laid off for reasons other than making a bad mistake is called "job security." Job security won't guarantee a raise or a promotion, but it will at least guarantee a job.

Conclusion

The energy market is the foundation of just about every other business there is. The people who work in the energy market are responsible for keeping our lights, heating systems, computers, televisions, stoves, ovens, and cars running. Think of all the things that would simply no longer work if the men and women in the energy sector decided to not show up for work one day!

The energy sector offers a wide range of careers. With so much to choose from, there just might be a career that would be a good fit for you!

Many of these jobs don't require a college education. Others can only be acquired with a college degree. When it comes to alternative energies, for example, many exciting careers are only available to

Wind farms create new jobs during their construction.

Wind Jobs

Once wind farms are working, they need:

- managers
- wind turbine technicians
- wind turbine maintenance workers
- administrative and office support

someone with a bachelor's or master's degree. Someone who goes to college to pursue a career in the energy market could learn anything from **meteorology** to engineering, from chemistry to physics. For someone truly interested in the science behind energy and fuel, college can be extremely valuable.

Looking at the Words

Meteorology is the study of weather patterns and climate.

That said, you can still make good money without a college degree. The question is: What's the best choice for you? What interests you most? What do you enjoy doing the most? How do you define success?

Each individual will answer these questions differently. The answers will guide your decisions in the future. Does your path to success include a college education? Or could you get there by another route?

Either way, the energy market has well-paying jobs for you!

Find Out More

In Books

Challoner, Jack. *DK Eyewitness Books: Energy*. New York: DK Children, 2012.

Gardener, Robert. *Energy: Green Science Projects about Solar, Wind, and Water Power (Team Green Science Projects)*. Berkeley Heights, N.J.: Enslow Publishers, 2011.

Zemlicka, Shannon. *From Oil to Gas (Start to Finish, Second Series: Everyday Products)*. Minneapolis, Minn.: Twenty-First Century Books, 2013.

On the Internet

EIA Energy Kids
www.eia.gov/kids

Energy Star Kids
www.energystar.gov/index.cfm?c=kids.kids_index

Kids and Energy
www.kids.esdb.bg/index.html

Bibliography

Hamilton, James. Bureau of Labor Statistics. "Careers in Solar Power" http://www.bls.gov/green/solar_power/ (accessed March 9, 2013).

Hamilton, James and Drew Liming. Bureau of Labor Statistics. "Careers in Wind Power" http://www.bls.gov/green/wind_energy/ (accessed March 9, 2013).

ONET OnLine. "Continuous Mining Machine Operators" http://www.onetonline.org/link/summary/47-5041.00 (accessed March 12, 2013).

ONET OnLine. "Crushing, Grinding, and Polishing Machine Setters, Operators, and Tenders" http://www.onetonline.org/link/summary/51-9021.00 (accessed March 12, 2013).

ONET OnLine. "Heavy and Tractor-Trailer Truck Drivers" http://www.onetonline.org/link/summary/53-3032.00 (accessed March 12, 2013).

ONET OnLine. "Mine Cutting and Channeling Machine Operators" http://www.onetonline.org/link/summary/47-5042.00 (accessed March 12, 2013).

ONET OnLine. "Power Plant Operators" http://www.onetonline.org/link/summary/51-8013.00 (accessed March 12, 2013).

ONET OnLine. "Tank Car, Truck, and Ship Loaders" http://www.onetonline.org/link/summary/53-7121.00 (accessed March 12, 2013).

PA Announcer. "So You Want to Be an Announcer." http://www.pa-announcer.com/pa_006.htm (accessed February 14, 2013).

U.S. Bureau of Labor Statistics. "Electricians" http://www.bls.gov/ooh/construction-and-extraction/electricians.htm (accessed March 11, 2013).

U.S. Bureau of Labor Statistics. "Mechanical Engineering Technicians." http://www.bls.gov/ooh/architecture-and-engineering/mechanical-engineering-technicians.htm (accessed March 11, 2013).

U.S. Bureau of Labor Statistics. "Oil and Gas Workers." http://www.bls.gov/ooh/construction-and-extraction/oil-and-gas-workers.htm (accessed March 11, 2013).

Index

About the Author

Connor Syrewicz is a writer and editor from Binghamton, New York. He was raised on Long Island, has a degree in English, and spends most of his time writing and facilitating other creative projects. His interests include art and philosophy, which he actively incorporates into his writing.

Picture Credits

banner: Lisa F. Young | Dreamstime; p. 6: NASA: p. 8: Eric Kounce, Texas Raiser; p. 12: Butler Community College; p. 14: BoH p. 16: Lisa F. Young | Dreamstime.com; p. 18: Markha40 | Dreamstime.com; p. 22: Kodyn | Dreamstime.com; p. 26: American Spirit | Dreamstime.com; p. 30: David Gaylor | Dreamstime.com; p. 32: Netwan Handoko Hasan | Dreamstime.com; p. 34: Andrew Mits | Dreamstime.com; p. 36: Butler Community College; p. 38: Lydur Sulason; p. 40: Storfix | Dreamstime.com; p. 42: Walter Siegmund; p. 43: Richard J. Brunson, U.S. Navy; pp. 44, 45: North Carolina Division of Water Quality; p. 46: Sakuma Power Plant; p. 47: Ed Brown; p. 48: Hagerty Ryan, U.S. Fish and Wildlife Service; p. 50: Dmitry Kalinovsky | Dreamstime.com; p. 52: Mrbrefast; p. 55: Stephen Friedt; p. 56: Mwomack91; p. 58: Philip May